Editor
Sara Connolly

Managing Editor
Ina Massler Levin, M.A.

Illustrator
Blanca Apodaca

Cover Artist
Tony Carrillo

Art Production Manager
Kevin Barnes

Imaging
Rosa C. See

Publisher
Mary D. Smith, M.S. Ed.

Grades 3–6

50 Book Report Ideas

Author

Jim Walters, M.A., N.B.C.T.

Teacher Created Resources, Inc.
6421 Industry Way
Westminster, CA 92683
www.teachercreated.com

ISBN-1-4206-3948-X

©2006 Teacher Created Resources, Inc.

Made in U.S.A.

Table of Contents

Alternative Ideas for Book Reporting
in Primary Grades
(can be adapted to other grades)
Rationale: Students are provided with several ways to respond to a reading selection, according to his/her favored learning style.

Strategy: Learning Centers

Differentiate What: Product

Differentiate How: Learning styles

Teacher Preparation:
Prepare the following four center activities for students:
1. Diorama
2. Filmstrip maker
3. Costume and Letter
4. Puppet making

Other centers may include: computer activities, word processing, poetry center, mobile-making, debate, or interviews.

Explanation: The student reads a self-selected selection or teacher-selected selction. Then the student completes a center activity in response to the literature/reading selection. The student has several choices to choose from depending upon the number of center stations/activities the teacher designs around the room. The following are four examples of ways that students could respond to a literature selection.

Diorama Center # 1

Student Outcome:
At this center you will be able to create a scene from the book you read using the materials provided by the teacher. The scene should show the *setting* from the story and *what happened* in the story.

Materials needed:
After reading a story or book, use the variety of materials provided in the MATERIALS BOX to make a scene inside the shoe box. You may use glue, scissors and tape. You may also bring in items from home to complete your diorama.

Procedure:
_____1. First, collect your materials for your diorama. (Get a few paper towels in case you spill any glue.
_____2. Next, work quietly to design a scene for inside the shoebox. The scene

needs to be from the story you read.

_____3. Then, place your shoebox diorama in a place to dry.

_____4. After that, clean your work area and return your materials to their proper places.

_____5. Finally, in your very best handwriting, write a paper telling about your diorama scene. Use this as a STARTER SENTENCE.

My diorama shows a scene from the story called:

_____

____. This scene is about

_____.

The reason I made this scene is because

_____

_____.

_____6. Place your paper in the FINISHED or NOT FINISHED folder.

_____7. Fill out an EVALUATION sheet and place it in the FINISHED folder.

Filmstrip Center #2

Student Outcome:
At this center you will create a filmstrip using the materials provided by the teacher. The filmstrip will tell about and show all the important elements of the story.

Materials needed:
small box, filmstrip paper, pencils, tape, and crayons or colored pencils.

Procedure:
_____1. Watch the teacher-made filmstrip that shows how to create your filmstrip.

_____2. Follow ALL the directions. Raise your hand if you need help.

_____3. Clean your work area and place your filmstrip in a safe place.

_____4. Fill out an EVALUATION sheet and place it in the FINISHED folder.

Costume and Letter Writing Center #3

Student Outcome:
At this center you are to select a favorite character from the story you read, plan a costume to make you look like your favorite character, and write a letter to your parents asking for help in dressing like your favorite character on Friday.

****

****

*

Date: _____

Dear _____,

   I just read a book called _____.

It was written by

_____.

The illustrations were drawn by

_____.

My favorite character in the story was

_____

because

_____.

   My teacher said that I have permission to dress like my favoite character this

Friday, _____. Would you please help me dress up like my

favorite character? Here is a list of things I thought I could use to help me dress up and look like my favorite character:

_____

_____

_____

_____.

Thanks!

                     Love,

                     _____

Fill out an EVALUATION sheet and place it in the FINISHED folder.

Puppet Making Center #4

Student Outcome:
At this center you will create puppet of one of the characters from the story or book you read, using the materials provided by the teacher.
(You may choose to make a puppet out of brown bags and newspaper, popsicle sticks and paper, or any other materials available to you in the materials box.)

Materials needed:
brown bag, newspaper, rubber band, popsicle sticks, yarn, construction paper, wiggly eyes, felt, glue, scissors, tape, etc.

Procedure:
_____1. Look at the puppet models provided. Decide what kind of puppet you would like to make. (You can create an original puppet).
_____2. Gather your materials from the "Materials Box" and make your puppet. (Raise your hand if you need help.)
_____3. Clean your work area and place your puppet in a safe place to dry.

_____4. Complete the "Paper Bag Reporting" sheet and attach it with tape to the back side of your paper bag puppet.

_____5. Fill out an EVALUATION sheet and place it in the FINISHED folder.

****
****

Paper Bag Reporting

This book is about _____

_____.

In the story, _____

_____.

My favorite part was when _____

_____.

My favorite character in the story was _____ because

_____.

I would say that this book is very _____

because _____.

Introduction

With *50 Book Report Ideas,* you will never run out of new ideas for book reports and literary projects. This teacher resource book contains 50 hands-on book report ideas with their own graphic organizers. It is designed for students who love new activities and teachers who don't have enough time to invent something new.

These reports go beyond typical one-page essays. Most of the projects can be done during class time and require materials found in every classroom—writing paper, construction paper, art supplies, and students' imaginations.

The ideas are appropriate for fiction, nonfiction, and even picture books. With these projects, students compare and contrast stories and characters, create time lines, design puzzles and trading cards, and even dress up as famous people from history. They pretend to be characters in the books they read, writing letters and creating scrapbooks. They grade characters on their behavior and pack suitcases for faraway travel.

Because the reports are appropriate for grades 3 through 6, students with various reading levels can complete the reports and projects successfully. Younger students can easily design book awards and story flags. More adventurous students might want to create junk drawer sculptures or give press conferences. There is sure to be a report appropriate for every student in the classroom.

At the back of the book are lists of Newbery Award Winners, California Young Reader Medal Winners, and Caldecott Medal Winners. Any of these books would be great choices for fantastic student book reports.

Animal Poster

Teacher Note: Have students use this book report for stories in which an animal is either the main character or one of the main characters. The report should not be used for a reference book about animals.

Materials

- Animal Poster Report Organizer (page 5)

- paper

- pencil or pen

- clothes hanger

- construction paper

- art supplies such as paint, cutouts, stitchery, yarn strips, felt pens, or crayons

Procedure

Your book report will be four paragraphs long. Use the Animal Report Organizer to help your plan it. Make sure that you write the first paragraph like an actual paragraph, and not like a list of information. Include the title, author, name of publisher, as well as the number of pages. Also, tell whether the book is from home, school, or the public library.

In the second paragraph, tell the plot of the story. Remember, the plot tells the main events of the story. Don't put in every detail. Write just enough to describe what is happening.

In the third paragraph, write about the animal's personality. How did the animal's personality affect the story? Did the animal do anything unusual or funny? Did you learn anything about the way an animal might think as a result of reading this book?

Your final paragraph will describe the relationship between the animals and any humans in the story. For example, in the story of *Winnie the Pooh*, there is a special bond between Winnie the Pooh and Christopher Robin. How would you describe the relationship in the book you read?

For the project portion of this report, you will make your own banner for the book. Use a hanger and attach a piece of construction paper to it. Decorate your banner with a picture about your story. You can use paint, paper, cutouts, stitchery, yarn strips, felt pens, or crayons.

Animal Poster *(cont.)*

Name _____ **Animal Poster Report Organizer**

Notes on first paragraph

Notes on second paragraph

Notes on third paragraph

Notes on fourth paragraph

Book Award

Materials

- Book Award Organizer (page 7)
- construction paper
- pencils
- scissors
- glue
- art supplies such as felt pens, crayons, or paint

Procedure

Some books are better than others, but you could say something good about every book in the library. For this report you are going to make and give an award to the book you read. Use the Book Award Organizer to help you plan your award.

First, take a half sheet of construction paper and draw the cover just the way you see it. The book cover picture and the award should be bold and bright. Start with light pencil lines and when you are satisfied, color them in. A good way to check what you've done is to look at your project from across the room. Can you easily read it? Does it look interesting? Are the words and pictures too small, too big, or just right? Looking from across the room helps you see what others see.

Use another sheet of construction paper to design an award for your book. Think about what kind of award you want to give your book. Here are some possibilities:

- Best book
- Most interesting characters
- Best illustrations
- Most chapters
- Best descriptions
- Biggest surprise in a book
- Great information
- Best in a series
- Best by this author
- Best action in a book
- Funniest book

Take out a full piece of construction paper and write your name and the date at the top. Glue your book cover onto this paper. Cut out your award and glue it beside the cover.

6

Book Award (cont.)

Name _____ **Book Award Organizer**

Practice on these awards before you design your award.

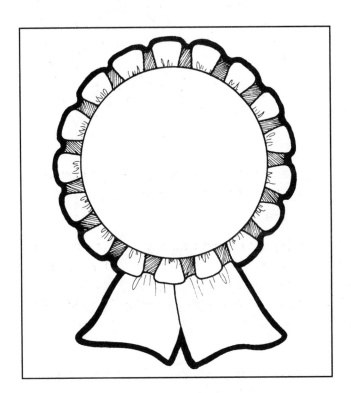

Book Brochure

> **Teacher Note:** For this book report, students should choose a book that takes place in another part of the world.

Materials

- Book Brochure Chart (page 9)
- 9" x 12" construction paper
- pencils or pens
- felt pens or crayons

Procedure

For this book report, you are going to create a brochure, or a pamphlet, describing the story you have just read. Use the Book Brochure Chart to help you plan your brochure.

Take a piece of 9" by 12" construction paper and fold it in half lengthwise. At the top of the front page, write the title of the book in bold letters. Write the author's name underneath the title. Below that, draw a large picture depicting the location where the story takes place. Write your name at the bottom of the page.

The inside of your brochure should be split into four parts. In the first part, you will draw a picture of the setting of the book and then write a description of it. Be sure to include good adjectives that get the reader interested in the book.

Below that, on the second part of the brochure, write about the characters. Make them come alive by writing about what they said and did, then draw a picture of them.

On the third part of the brochure, describe the problem the characters faced in the book. Draw a picture to illustrate your writing.

On the fourth part, write about how the characters solved the problem they faced. Draw a picture of that as well.

Remember to make the book sound as interesting as you can. You want other students to read the book because you have made it sound so interesting. You will be presenting your brochure to the class.

Book Brochure *(cont.)*

Name _____ **Book Brochure Chart**

Use this graphic organizer to plan your brochure.

Front Page   **Inside Page**

| Title Author's Name |
| Picture |

| Drawing and Description of Setting |
| Describe the characters |

| Problem |
| Solution |

CD Album Cover

Teacher Note: For this book report students should choose any book that has only one story in it.

Materials

- CD Album Cover Organizer (page 11)
- 11" x 5" light cardboard
- art supplies such as pens or crayons
- tape

Procedure

Fold the 11" by 5" cardboard in half widthwise and tape the edges so that it looks like a CD album case.

Use the CD Album Cover Organizer to design the front of your album. Include the title of the book in your design. Use only the amount of information you need to get someone interested in owning the album. Don't overdo the front. Make your design as bold and large as possible. When you are happy with your design, draw it on the front of the cardboard.

Use the CD Album Cover Organizer to brainstorm a summary of the plot that will make someone want to buy the CD. Use no more than five sentences. Then think of 10 song titles that could be inspired by the story. You should make these titles up. However, you may use existing songs if you wish.

Write your summary and song titles on the back of the cardboard. At the bottom of the cardboard, write the name of the company that makes the album. This company will naturally be named after you.

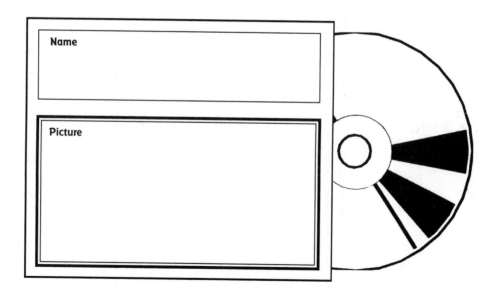

CD Album Cover (cont.)

Name _____ **CD Album Cover Organizer**

Design the front and back of your album here

Name

Picture

Front Page

Back Page

Summary

Song Titles

Name of Company

Character Can

Materials

- Character Can Organizer (page 13)

- coffee can

- art supplies such as construction paper, yarn, ribbon, pens, crayons, scissors, and glue

- 1" x 3" strips of paper

Procedure

Choose one character from your book. Fill out the Character Can Organizer to brainstorm what you learned about the character.

On each of the strips of paper, write a sentence about your character. Use your organizer to help you think of as many sentences as you can.

Use your art supplies to decorate the coffee can. Make it look like your character or like your character's head.

Place the sentence strips inside the coffee can.

12

Character Can *(cont.)*

Name _____   **Character Can Organizer**

Name of your character:

_____

_____

_____

Things your character did in the story:

_____

_____

Reasons why this character was important to the story:

_____

_____

_____

Three things that made this character unusual:

_____

_____

_____

One thing you learned from this character:

_____

_____

_____

Your favorite thing about this character:

_____

_____

_____

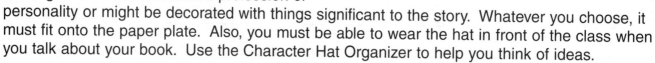

Character Hat

Teacher Note: Students should choose a fiction or nonfiction book in which the main character stands out. Examples of books like this are the following:

Strega Nona by Tomie dePaola

Sarah, Plain and Tall by Patricia MacLachlan

Lon Po Po: A Red-Riding Hood Story from China by Ed Young

Somebody and the Three Bears by Marilyn Tolhurst

Sylvester and the Magic Pebble by William Steig

Materials

- Character Hat Organizer (page 15)
- paper plate
- art supplies such as construction paper, pens, crayons, glue, and scissors

Procedure

For this book report you should choose a fiction or nonfiction book in which the main character really stands out.

After you have read the book, you will create a paper plate hat that your character might wear. The hat might show the character's profession or personality or might be decorated with things significant to the story. Whatever you choose, it must fit onto the paper plate. Also, you must be able to wear the hat in front of the class when you talk about your book. Use the Character Hat Organizer to help you think of ideas.

When you give your report to the class, you will tell the class what this character did in the story and why the character was important to the book. You will need to list at least three things that make the character unusual. Tell one thing you learned from what he or she did, and one thing that you could do better than him or her.

Character Hat *(cont.)*

Name _____ **Character Hat Organizer**

Things you could put on your hat:

_____

_____

Things your character did in the story:

_____

_____

Reasons why this character was important to the story:

_____

_____

Three things that made this character unusual:

_____

_____

One thing you learned from this character:

_____

_____

One thing you can do better than this character:

_____

_____

Character Mask

Teacher Note: This report should be done for a book with a central main character.

Materials

- Character Mask Organizer (page 17)
- art supplies such as paper plates, construction paper, cardboard, pens, crayons, scissors, and glue

Procedure

Use the Character Mask Organizer to brainstorm information about your book and your character. Then write a two-paragraph report about the book.

The first paragraph of your report should be written like a paragraph and not just a list of information. Include the title, author, name of publisher, as well as the number of pages. Also, include whether the book is from home, school, or the public library.

The second paragraph should describe the main character. Include what the person is like, what he or she did, and how they looked. What things do you like about this character? Is there something he or she did that reminds you of yourself or someone else you know? Write about that, too.

Use your art supplies to create a mask depicting your favorite book character. You can use construction paper, cardboard, or any other material you like. You are going to hold the mask over your face while you read your report to the class, so be sure to cut out a space for your mouth so that your classmates can hear you speak.

Character Mask *(cont.)*

Name _____ **Character Mask Organizer**

Information about your book:

Title:_____

Author:_____

Publisher: _____

Number of pages: _____

Where you got the book:_____

Information about your main character:

What she/he was like? _____

_____

What did she/he do? _____

_____

How did this character look?_____

_____

Things you liked about this character: _____

_____

Things about this person that remind you of someone else:

_____

_____

_____

_____

Character Wanted Poster

Materials

- Character Wanted Poster Organizer (page 19)

- pens or crayons

- scissors

- construction paper

Procedure

For this book report you may choose any book that has only one main character. This assignment is designed to show others how well you understood that person. You are going to be able to do this by creating a "Character Wanted Poster."

Think about how you want your poster to look and what you want it to say. You will want to include a picture of the person and then describe him or her. You might also want to include these things:

- Name of character

- Height

- Hair color

- Weight

- Eye color

- Distinguishing features (scars, birthmarks)

- Date last seen

- Wanted for

- Reward amount

- Contact person (your name)

Character Wanted Poster *(cont.)*

Name _____ **Character Wanted Poster Organizer**

Information about your book:

Character's Name _____

Height _____ Weight _____

Hair Color _____ Eye Color _____

Scars or Birthmarks _____

Wanted for _____ Reward Amount _____

Your Message

Character's Name

Picture

Crime

Children as Main Characters

> **Teacher Note:** This book report is for a story with a child as the main character or one of the main characters.

Materials

- Children as Main Characters Chart (pg. 21)

- 3" by 36" strip of butcher paper

- pencil

- art materials such as colored pencils, crayons, or watercolor pens

Procedure

If you have ever read *The Great Brain*, *Little House on the Prairie*, or *The Adventures of Winnie the Pooh*, then you have read a book with a child as a main character. Do you relate to these main characters more than you would if the character was an adult or an animal?

Sometimes when you read books like these, you might see pictures of the scenes in your mind, like a movie. For this book report, you will draw a "movie" of your book and present it to the class. Use the Children as Main Characters Chart to help you plan your movie.

Here's how you make your movie:

1. Cut a long strip of butcher paper 3" by 36"

2. Roll each of the ends around a pencil.

3. Tape the ends to the pencils.

4. Before you begin drawing, write the name of the book, the author, the publisher, the number of pages, and your name.

5. Then use crayons, colored pencils, or watercolor pens to draw three or four scenes that tell the story.

6. Roll your movie up around the pencils.

7. Tell the story to the class.

Children as Main Characters *(cont.)*

Name _____ **Children as Main Characters Chart**

Write out four events from the story in this chart. Use this chart to help you design your movie.

1

2

3

4

Cinderella T-Chart

Teacher Note: For this book report, students will read a traditional version of Cinderella as well as a story that is very similar—perhaps from a different culture. There are hundreds of other books that have the same story line but are presented differently. Some versions can even be found on the Internet.

Some possible books are

The Egyptian Cinderella by Shirley Climo. HarperCollins, 1993.

The Korean Cinderella by Shirley Climo. HarperCollins, 1993.

Mufaro's Beautiful Daughters by John Steptoe. Scholastic, 1987.

Princess Furball, by Charlotte Huck. Greenwillow Books, 1989.

The Rough-Face Girl by Rafe Martin. Putnam's, 1992.

Tattercoats: An Old English Tale by Flora Annie Stelle. Bradbury Press, 1976.

Vasilisa the Beautiful by Thomas P. Whitney. Macmillan, 1970.

Yeh-Shen: A Cinderella Story from China by Ai-Ling Louie. Philomel Books, 1982.

Materials

- Cinderella T-Chart (page 23)
- *Cinderella* (traditional version)
- another version of *Cinderella*

Procedure

For this book report you are going to read two books—*Cinderella* and another book that's very much like it.

Read the stories. Then use your T-chart to compare the stories. List at least 10 facts about the stories. The example below will help you get started.

Cinderella	Mufaro's Beautiful Daughters
Takes place in France	Takes place in Africa
She has two stepsisters	There are only two daughters
One character is expected to serve the others	One character is expected to serve the others

Cinderella T-Chart *(cont.)*

Name _____ **Cinderella T-Chart**

Book #1 *Cinderella*	Book #2 Title: _____

Cinquain Poetry

Materials

• Cinquain Poetry Work Sheet (page 25)

Procedure

Cinquain poems are unrhymed poems that must have the right number of syllables in each line. They work like this:

Line 1: Two syllables or one word that gives the title

Line 2: Four syllables or two words describing something or someone

Line 3: Six syllables or three words telling an action

Line 4: Eight syllables or four words expressing a feeling

Line 5: Two syllables or another word for the title

Example

Boys

They are awesome

Always a thinkin'

Of some trouble to get into.

Boys, yea!

Now, you try writing one about the main character in your book. Practice writing your cinquain here, then write the final version on your work sheet for the class to see.

Your Name _____   Title _____

Author _____   Publisher _____

_____

_____

_____

_____

_____

Cinquain Poetry *(cont.)*

grass

cool, green

growing, swaying, standing

a great place to play games outdoors

fun

First Line: two syllables or one word giving title

Second Line: four syllables or two words describing title

Third Line: six syllables or three words expressing action

Fourth Line: eight syllables or four words expressing a feeling

Fifth Line: two syllables or another word for the title

Title of Poem _____

Author's Name _____

_____

_____, _____

_____, _____, _____

_____, _____, _____, _____

_____

Cluster/Word Web

Teacher Note: For this report students should choose a book that has more than one character. Examples of this type of book could be one of the following:

Charlotte's Web by E.B. White

Little House in the Big Woods
 by Laura Ingalls Wilder

The Courage of Sarah Noble by Alice Dalgliesh

Matilda by Roald Dahl

Caddie Woodlawn by Carol Ryrie Brink

Materials

- Cluster/Word Web (page 27)

Procedure

For this book report, you are going to create a cluster word graph showing how each of the characters in your book is different. You will need to write about four different characters.

To start, take out your Cluster/Word Web. Write the title, the author's name, and the publisher's name in the center circle. In each of the circles connecting to the center circle, write one character's name.

In the smallest circles, write two things about each character that makes him or her different from all the others.

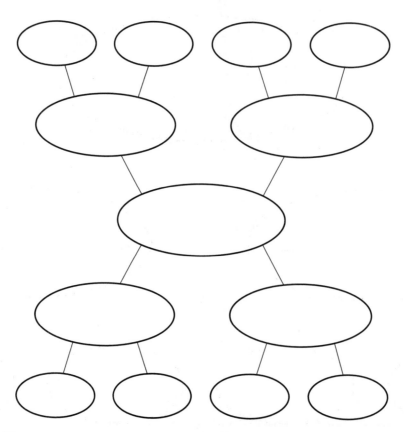

Cluster/Word Web *(cont.)*

Name _____**Cluster/Word Web**

Write the title, the author's name, and the publisher's name in the center circle. In each of the circles connecting to the center circle, write one character's name. Then write two things about each character that make him or her different from the others.

Collage

Materials

- Story Collage Chart (page 29)
- 9" x 12" construction paper
- arts and craft supplies
- scissors
- glue
- 1" x 6" label

Procedure

A collage is artwork that is made of a variety of art materials glued onto a surface. In this book report, you will be creating a collage of a chapter or scene from the book that you read.

Before you create your collage, you will write a two-paragraph report about your book. This will help you to think of some ideas to illustrate for your collage. Use your Story Collage chart to help you brainstorm the main events and the main characters of the story.

First, write a two-paragraph report about your book. The first paragraph should be written like a paragraph, not a list of information. It should include the title, author, name of publisher, and the number of pages; and whether the book is from home, school, or the public library.

In the second paragraph you will describe the main events of the story and introduce the main characters.

Finally, using arts and crafts supplies, you will put together a collage based on a character or even a scene in your book. Paste your collage onto a piece of 9" x 12" construction paper.

Place a label that is at least 1" x 6" on your collage. On it, write your name, the title of the book, and the author of the book.

Collage *(cont.)*

Name _____**Story Collage Chart**

Main events of the story:

Event #1 _____

Event #2 _____

Event #3 _____

Event #4 _____

Event #5 _____

Words that describe the main characters:

Character #1 _____   Name _____

Character #2 _____   Name _____

Character #3 _____   Name _____

Character #4 _____   Name _____

Character #5 _____   Name _____

Commercial

> **Teacher Note:** This report should be done for a fiction book.

Materials

- Design a Commercial Chart (page 31)
- props, costumes, or music (optional)

Procedure

When we go to the movies, we know that what we see isn't real, and that's okay. Commercials are different. They have people telling you to do or try something that is new to you. Commercials tell you what to think not simply through words, but everything in them that you hear and see. Sometimes they use music to make people want to buy their products.

For this report, you will write a commercial about the book that you read. You will try to "sell" it to the other students in your class to make them want to read it. You may want to use other people, props, or costumes in your commercial. You can even use music.

You must include the name of the book, the author's name, publisher, and number of pages in your commercial. Use the Design a Commercial Chart to help you plan the beginning, middle, and end of your commercial. The time limit may be any length you want, but should probably be between two and three minutes.

30

Commercial *(cont.)*

Name _____ **Design a Commercial Chart**

- Write notes in each section

Beginning

Middle

End

Comparing/Contrasting

Materials

- Compare/Contrast Chart (page 33)

Procedure

For this book report you are going to compare and contrast two characters. They can be from the same book, from two books by the same author books, or even from different books. We all remember *Frog and Toad*. If you were going to create a Comparing/Contrast Map of the characters of Frog and Toad, you would show how they are both alike (comparing) and yet very different (contrasting).

Use the Compare/Contrast Chart to brainstorm some ideas for your map.

Draw a Compare/Contrast map like the one below. On the left, describe how character #1 is different. Do the same for character #2 on the right. In the middle, describe how they are alike.

At the top of your page include this information:

Your Name: _____

Title _____   Author _____

Title _____   Author _____

Alike

Name   Name

Comparing/Contrasting *(cont.)*

Name _____ **Compare/Contrast Chart**

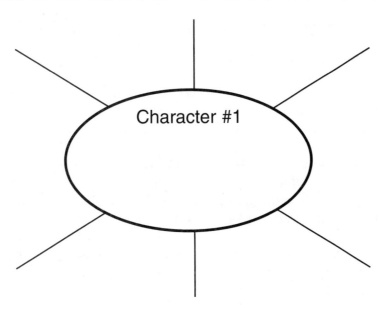

Character #1

How They Are Alike

_____

_____

_____

_____

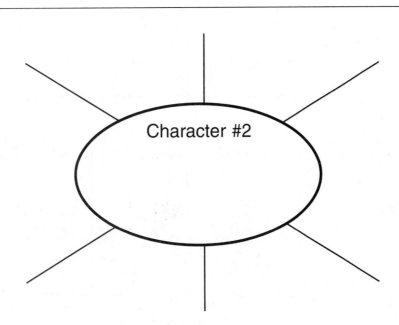

Character #2

Create a Quilt

Materials

- 12" x 12" construction paper

- art supplies such as crayons, colored pens, or colored pencils

Procedure

Your book report is going to be a part of a class project. Each member of the class is going to create one square of a classroom quilt. This quilt will be made up of construction paper squares.

On the 12" x 12" construction paper, draw a scene from your book. This could be a scene you liked, a scene that made you think, or the scene that you remembered best from the book. You can even draw your favorite character if you can't think of a scene. Make sure your square is brightly colored—you want it to be easily seen from across the room.

Make sure that at the top of the square you add your name, the title of the book, the author's name, and the publisher's name.

Create a Quilt *(cont.)*

Name _____ **Quilt Planning Chart**

Plan your quilt square here.

Culture Can

> **Teacher Note:** This report should be done for a fiction book about someone from a culture different from the student's.

Materials

- Culture Can Chart (page 37)

- an empty, cleaned out can such as a coffee can

- art supplies such as construction paper, glue, scissors, colored pens, and crayons

- at least five strips of 1" x 4" paper

Procedure

We often see people who are different than we are. It's natural to wonder about their lives and sometimes to even make a judgment about them based on what we see. Your assignment for this book report is to find a fiction book about someone from a culture other than your own. You will create a culture can and write a four-paragraph report about the book.

Use the Culture Can Chart to help you plan your report.

The first paragraph should be written like a paragraph, not a list of information. It should include the title, author, name of publisher, and the number of pages. Also, indicate whether the book is from home, school, or the public library.

The second paragraph will describe all the factual information you can find about the main character. Include the country where the person came from, approximately how long he or she has been in this country, and the things that you find different about the way this person looks, acts, or thinks.

Paragraph three will be your longest. Here you will describe the main events of the person's life. If a friend reads this paragraph, he or she will know about this character in the story. Don't write about all the little details—just the main things that happened.

Your last paragraph will explain what you thought of the book. As you write, you might think about what you learned from the book. Did your opinion of the character change when you finished the book? Did you like the book?

After you have finished your written report, you will decorate the coffee can (or whatever kind of can you have) with the flag of the country where the book took place. On the construction paper, draw and color the country's flag. Then paste the flag around the can.

Take out the strips of paper and write on each one a fact about the country. Place the strips of paper inside the can.

Culture Can *(cont.)*

Name _____ **Culture Can Chart**

Notes on the 1st paragraph

Notes on the 2nd paragraph

Notes on the 3rd paragraph

Notes on the 4th paragraph

Diamante Poetry

Materials

- Diamante Poetry Page (page 39)

Procedure

Diamante poems are unrhymed poems that are written in the shape of a diamond. They look like this:

Line 1. One noun giving the title

Line 2. Two adjectives describing the title

Line 3. Three words that end with "ed" or "ing" that describe the title

Line 4. Four nouns that are related to the title

Line 5. Three words that end with "ed" or "ing" that describe line 7

Line 6. Two adjectives that describe line 7

Line 7. One noun (the opposite of the title)

Here are some examples:

Girls
Smart, pretty
Playing, laughing, giggling
Growth, change, knowledge, development
Working, achieving, succeeding
Older, wiser
Adult

By Ivan

Mountain
High, rocky
Flying, looking, killing
Eagle, power, fear, rabbit
Living, moving, making noise
Deep, beautiful
Valley

By Amy

Rectangle
simple, conventional
using, measuring, balancing
boxes, rooms, desks, paper
holding, storing, enclosing
round, continuous
circle

Now, you try writing one about the main character in your book. When you finish here, write it on your Diamante Poetry Page for the class to see. Include your name, the title of the book, the author's name, and the publisher's name at the top.

Diamante Poetry *(cont.)*

Name _____ **Diamante Poetry Page**

Title of Book: _____

Author's Name: _____

Publisher's Name: _____

Title of Poem: _____

_____

_____, _____

_____, _____, _____

_____, _____, _____, _____

_____, _____, _____

_____, _____

_____

Dress Up Day

Teacher Note: This book report should be done on a biography.

Materials

- Dress Up Day Chart (page 41)
- costume depicting the subject of biography
- index cards

Procedure

For this book report, you will read a biography. A biography tells the story of a person's life. Pay close attention to what you learn about the subject of the biography because you are going to pretend to be that person when you present your report to the class. You will need to have some sort of costume that represents the person in your book. For example, if your biography was about Abraham Lincoln, you could come to class wearing a stovepipe hat.

You will also need to develop 10 cards that give facts about the person without giving away his or her name. When you present your report to the class, you will read these facts. The class then will play 20 questions trying to guess who you are. Here is an example of possible facts:

Possible facts about Abraham Lincoln:

- I was born very poor.
- I lived in a log cabin.
- My mother died when I was young.
- I became the president of the United States.
- Many people didn't like me when I was president.
- Some people even thought I looked ugly.
- I wanted to find a way to get rid of slavery.
- I led our country through the great Civil War.
- I was the 16th president.
- I was shot and killed while I was president.

Use the Dress Up Day Facts page to list some facts that you learned from the book. Then write these facts on index cards. Remember, don't use the person's name when you are writing the facts. Write them as if you were the person talking about yourself.

Dress Up Day *(cont.)*

Name _____ **Dress Up Day Chart**

Write your facts about the person's life and achievements here.

Fact 1
Fact 2
Fact 3
Fact 4
Fact 5
Fact 6
Fact 7
Fact 8
Fact 9
Fact 10

Event Timeline

Teacher Note: This report should be done on a book that takes place over a period of time.

Materials

- Time Line Chart (page 43)

- paper

- art supplies such as colored pencils, colored pens, or crayons

Procedure

For this book report you are going to read a story that takes place over a period of time and then make a timeline of all the events. Think about the important events that took place in the book. Use your Time Line Chart to write about these events in the order they occurred.

Take out a piece of paper. Start out by writing your name, the title of the book, the author's name, and the publisher's name. Next, create a timeline like the one below. On the left, write when the event happened. For example, was it in the morning or at night? Maybe it was a particular time of the year like spring or even a given month. Sometimes the book doesn't say when events happened. If that is the case then just say "beginning," "middle," or "ending."

Next, create a box at the end of each line and use your art supplies to draw pictures that illustrate each event.

Example Event Timeline

Morning   Alexander woke up and didn't want to go to school.

Event Timeline *(cont.)*

Name _____

Time Line Chart

Date

Historical Interview

Materials

- Historical Interview Chart (page 45)

Procedure

You are going to read a book about a famous character. This might be a fictional character or an actual person. As you read the book, think about how the character or person's life was different from the life you live.

On your Historical Interview Chart, write a list of things that were different about the person or character's life or the world in general at the time the person or character lived. You might find that he or she ate different foods, wore different clothing, or traveled in a way that you have never seen.

Next, you are going to interview a parent, grandparent, or an older adult about his or her life when he or she was young. Ask this person about what the world was like when he or she was growing up, what foods were popular, what clothing was worn, and what form of travel was the most popular.

Was the life of your family member or adult similar to the person you read about? How was it different? On your Historical Interview Chart, list seven ways that the person you interviewed was alike or different from the person you read about.

Historical Interview *(cont.)*

Name _____ **Historical Interview Chart**

How your Character's Life Was Different

1. _____

2. _____

3. _____

4. _____

5. _____

6. _____

7. _____

How Your Ancestor's Life Compared:

1. _____

2. _____

3. _____

4. _____

5. _____

6. _____

7. _____

Historical Fiction Book Cover

Materials

- Notes for Historical Fiction Report (page 47)
- art supplies such as construction paper, gift-wrapping paper, comic pages, paper bags, colored pens, colored pencils, crayons, scissors, and glue

Procedure

For this book report, you are to read an historical fiction book. This is simply a fiction story that happened sometime in history. It could be at any time in history—it just can't take place in the present time.

First, you are going to write a four-paragraph report about the book. Use the Notes for Historical Fiction Report page to help you plan your report.

The first paragraph should be written like a paragraph, not a list of information. It will include the title, author, name of publisher, as well as the number of pages. Also, indicate whether the book is from home, school, or the public library.

The second paragraph will tell all the factual information you can find about the main character. Include the person's birthday, place of birth, who he or she married, and how many children he or she had.

Paragraph three will be your longest. Here you will tell the main events of the person's life—not all the little details. When other people read this paragraph, they will know about the character's life.

In the fourth paragraph, you will tell what you thought of the book. Did you like it? What did you like most (or least)? Did your character do anything that you thought was unusual?

Now you are going to design a book cover for the historical fiction book that you read. You can be creative and have some fun. Draw the character, the setting, or even a scene from the book—anything you want. You may use construction paper, gift-wrapping paper, comic pages, paper bags, or anything else you can think of. Make sure that somewhere on your cover you include the title of the book, the author's name, the publisher's name, and—don't forget—your name.

Historical Fiction Book Cover (cont.)

Name _____ **Notes for Historical Fiction Report**

Notes on the 1st paragraph

Notes on the 2nd paragraph

Notes on the 3rd paragraph

Notes on the 4th paragraph

Junk Drawer Sculpture

Teacher Note: This book report should be done on a book about an artist.

Materials

- Junk Drawer Chart (page 49)
- "junk drawer" supplies
- string, tape, or a hot glue gun

Procedure

You are going to read a book about an artist. Many people in the world make their living by being artists. Some paint, some perform, and others sculpt. (Sculpting is creating a statue of some kind.)

For this report, you will write a four-paragraph report about the book and then you will create a sculpture about the artist. To create your sculpture, you will use items from your junk drawer at home. Have you ever noticed that most people have a junk drawer at home? It's the place where your family keeps all sorts of supplies that don't fit anywhere else, like scissors, screws, nails, glue, paper, pens, and much, much more. Make sure that you get permission from your parents before using the contents of your junk drawer. They will probably be happy to let you clean some stuff out of there!

First, you will write your report. The first paragraph should be written like a paragraph, not a list of information. Include the title, the author's name, the publisher's name, and the number of pages. Also, indicate whether the book is from home, school, or the public library.

The second paragraph will tell all the factual information you can find about the artist. Include the year and the country where he or she was born, what kind of artwork he or she does (or did), and your opinion of the artwork.

Paragraph three will be your longest. Here you will tell the main events of the person's life. If a friend reads this paragraph, he or she will know about this artist in the story. Don't write about all the little details—just the main events. Finally, your last paragraph will tell what you thought of the book. Did you like it? What did you learn? Did your opinion of this type of art change when you finished the book?

Now, using the contents of the "junk drawer" at home, create a sculpture based on the artist in your book. Use the Junk Drawer Chart to list the supplies you find and how you will assemble them. This sculpture must be under 12" tall and no more than 8" wide. You can connect your items with string, tape, or, if you'd like, a hot glue gun.

Junk Drawer Sculpture *(cont.)*

Name _____**Junk Drawer Chart**

Supplies I will need:

hot glue gun _____

glue _____

cardboard _____

junk items _____

Parent's Permission _____

Assembly

1st _____

2nd _____

3rd _____

4th _____

5th _____

6th _____

7th _____

8th _____

9th _____

10th _____

Letter to the Author

Teacher Note: This report should be done on a book with only one story.

Materials

- Letter to Author Planning Page (page 51)
- paper

Procedure

For this assignment you may choose any book that has only one story.

In this book report you will write a letter to the author asking questions and giving your comments about the book. Tell the author what you thought of the book. Did it remind you of anything that has happened to you? Did you want to know more about the character? What did you want to know? When you were reading the story did you see something that was like an event that happened in the world somewhere? Many times authors will have a recurring theme running through their books. Did you notice anything that you've read before in another of the author's books? Is this book similar to another book you've read? Tell the author how you connected his or her book to your life, the world, or another book.

Use the Letter to Author Planning Page to plan what you will write in your letter. Write your actual letter on another piece of paper. Make sure that you use proper letter format with the five elements. There should be a date, a greeting, the body of the letter, a closing, and your signature.

Letter to the Author *(cont.)*

Name _____**Letter to Author Planning Page**

_____
Date

_____
Greeting

_____

_____

_____

_____

_____

_____

_____

_____

_____
Closing

_____
Signature

Musical

Materials

- My Book Report Song (page 53)

Procedure

For this book report, you will read a book of your choice and write a song about it. Use the same tune as "Old MacDonald Had a Farm." Here's how to do it:

1. <u>Old</u> <u>Mac</u> <u>Donald</u> <u>had</u> <u>a</u> <u>farm</u>

2. <u>E</u> <u>I</u> <u>E</u> <u>I</u> <u>O</u>

3. <u>And</u> <u>on</u> <u>that</u> <u>farm</u> <u>he</u> <u>had</u> <u>a</u> <u>pig</u>

4. <u>E</u> <u>I</u> <u>E</u> <u>I</u> <u>O</u>

5. <u>With</u> <u>an</u> <u>oink</u> <u>oink</u> <u>here</u>

6. <u>And</u> <u>an</u> <u>oink</u> <u>oink</u> <u>there</u>

7. <u>Here</u> <u>an</u> <u>oink,</u> <u>there</u> <u>an</u> <u>oink</u>

8. <u>Everywhere</u> <u>an</u> <u>oink</u> <u>oink</u>

9. <u>Old</u> <u>Mac</u> <u>Donald</u> <u>had</u> <u>a</u> <u>farm</u>

10. <u>E</u> <u>I</u> <u>E</u> <u>I</u> <u>O</u>

After you have read your book, write your song by filling in the spaces on the next page. It's as simple as that. As you write, sing it in your head to the tune of "Old MacDonald." Be prepared to sing it for the class or have a friend help you. Good luck!

Musical _(cont.)_

Name: _____**My Book Report Song**

Name of Book _____

Author _____ Number of pages _____

Publisher_____ Illustrator _____

1. _____ _____ _____ _____ _____

2. _____ _____ _____ _____

3. _____ _____ _____ _____ _____ _____

4. _____ _____ _____ _____

5. _____ _____ _____ _____

6. _____ _____ _____ _____

7. _____ _____ _____ _____ _____

8. _____ _____ _____

9. _____ _____ _____ _____ _____

10. _____ _____ _____ _____

Mystery Puzzle

Teacher Note: This report should be done on a mystery book. Some possible books are the following:

The Eleventh Hour: A Curious Mystery by Graeme Base

Julius, the Baby of the World by Kevin Henkes

King Bidgood's in the Bathtub by Audrey Wood

Somebody and the Three Blairs by Marilyn Tolhurst

Tacky the Penguin by Helen Lester

Tar Beach by Faith Ringgold

Materials

- Mystery Puzzle Planning Page (page 55)
- lightweight cardboard or heavy paper
- re-closeable plastic bag
- scissors
- art supplies such as glue, colored pens, colored pencils, or crayons

Procedure

This book report is to be done on a mystery book. First, you will write a two-paragraph report about your book. Then, you will create a puzzle showing how the book ends.

Use the Mystery Puzzle Planning Page to plan your two-paragraph report.

Your first paragraph should be written like a paragraph, not a list of information. It should include the title, the author's name, the publisher's name, and the number of pages. Also, tell whether the book is from home, school, or the public library.

In the second paragraph you will describe the main events of the mystery. But don't tell how it ends! Your puzzle will do that for you.

After you have finished your written report, you will create your puzzle to show the ending of the book. Show the solution as best you can. Follow these steps:

1. Draw and color a picture.
2. Glue the picture to lightweight cardboard or heavy paper
3. On the back, draw up to six interlocking puzzle pieces
4. Cut the puzzle out along the lines you drew.
5. Put the pieces in your re-closeable plastic bag

Mystery Puzzle *(cont.)*

Name _____**Mystery Puzzle Planning Page**

Notes on the First Paragraph

Title _____

Author's Name _____

Publisher _____

Number of Pages _____

Where you got this book _____

Notes on the Second Paragraph

Event #1 _____

Event #2 _____

Event #3 _____

Event #4 _____

Event #5 _____

Event #6 _____

News Article

> **Teacher Note:** This report should be done on a nonfiction book that describes an event that took place in the past.

Materials

- Five Ws Chart (page 57)

- paper

- black pen

- black-and-white photograph (optional)

Procedure

For this book report you may choose a nonfiction book that describes an event that took place in the past. Remember the five "W" questions as you read:

✔ What happened?	✔ When did it happen?
✔ Who was there?	✔ Where did it happen?
✔ Why did it happen?	

Use the Five Ws Chart to write your answers to these questions.

Now, rewrite the story as though it was a news article. At the top of your article write a catchy headline. Somewhere in your report include a black and white photograph or drawing.

Remember, this newspaper article needs to be a quick retelling of the whole story, so try to develop short paragraphs that answer only one of the questions above. Don't worry if you have to repeat a piece of information you've already used in another paragraph.

Make your report look like a newspaper by printing it nicely. You will also present your report to the class.

News Article *(cont.)*

Name _____ **Five Ws Chart**

- Fill in each row with details that answer the question.

What happened?
Who was there?
Why did it happen?
When did it happen?
Where did it happen?

Paper Bag Puppet

Materials

- Paper Bag Puppet Story Chart (page 59)

- small paper lunch bag

- art supplies such as colored pens, colored pencils, crayons, paper, scissors, and glue

Procedure

This book must be one with a main character. This character could be a person or an animal. You are going to create a paper bag puppet of the character to tell his or her story.

Lay the paper bag flat with the folded bottom facing up. The flap made by the bottom fold will be the mouth. On a piece of paper, draw the character's head. You may also choose to draw the character's arms and legs, as well as anything this person might hold or wear. Color and cut out your pieces, and then glue them onto the bag.

Your character should have bold and bright colors. Start with light pencil lines and when you are satisfied, color them in. A good way to see if you like what you've done is to look at your project from across the room. Are the features of the face too small? Can you easily tell what the puppet is? Are you proud of what you've done? This helps you see what others see.

Next, use the Paper Bag Puppet Story Chart to write an outline of the story that you can follow when you present your report to the class. This is your opportunity to make the book come alive for the class. Be sure to include all the most interesting parts of the story. You might want to find some dialogue from this person and read it. Whatever you say, it must be from this person's point of view.

Paper Bag Puppet *(cont.)*

Name _____**Paper Bag Puppet Story Chart**

Write notes in each section.

Setting: Time: Place:

↓

Characters:

↓

Problem:

↓ ↔

Plot/Events:

Resolution:

Paper Dolls

Teacher Note: This book report should be done on any book with several main characters.

Materials

- Paper Doll Pattern (page 61)
- legal-sized paper
- scissors
- art supplies such as colored pens, colored pencils, or crayons
- construction paper
- glue

Procedure

For this book report you may choose any book that has several main characters.

After you have read this book, you are going to create a string of four paper dolls by cutting out a shape using the Paper Doll Pattern. Here's how you do it:

1. Fold the legal-sized paper into four equal parts. Make sure your folds are very straight and tight.

2. Hold the Paper Doll Pattern over your folded paper. Make sure that the hands of the patterns are touching the very edges of the paper.

3. Cut out the shape. You will have a string of paper dolls connected at the hands. If they fell apart, then you didn't make sure the hands touched the edge of the paper.

These paper dolls are going to represent the different characters in your book. Use your art supplies to draw faces, hair, skin colors, and clothes. Make them all look as different as you can.

Mount the paper dolls on a piece of construction paper. At the top of the page write your name, the title of the book, and the author's name. Underneath that, write the name of the publisher and the name of the illustrator.

Under each character write a short description of that person. Describe what they did in the story and why they are important to the story.

Paper Dolls *(cont.)*

Paper Doll Pattern

Use this basic shape or make one of your own.

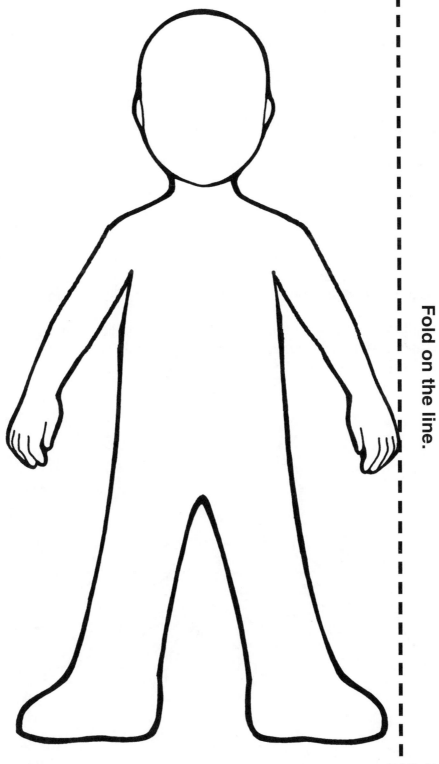

Fold on the line.

Paper Plate

> **Teacher Note:** This report is for a story with an animal as the main character or as one of the main characters. It should not be a reference book about animals.

Materials

- Paper Plate Patterns (page 62)
- paper plate
- scissors
- glue (or tape or a stapler)
- art supplies such as colored pens, colored pencils, crayons, and construction paper
- googly eyes (optional)

Procedure

For this book report, you will read a story with an animal as the main character or one of the main characters. After you read the story, you will be recreating that animal using a paper plate. Practice some ideas for your design using the Paper Plate Pattern.

Use your art supplies to make the paper plate look as much like your animal as you can. Be creative, but make sure it can be recognized as your animal. Your design can be freestanding, a mask, wall hanging, or a puppet. Use your imagination.

Paper Plate *(cont.)*

Name _____ **Paper Plate Patterns**

Try your hand at creating a face using the patterns below.

Idea # 31

People Who Changed the World

Teacher Note: This book report is for a book about an inventor, world leader, or educator.

Materials

- People Who Changed the World Chart (page 65)

- art supplies such as paper, colored pens, colored pencils, crayons, scissors, and glue

Procedure

Inventors, world leaders, and educators are all people who have changed the world. For this book report you are going to read about one of these people who made a real difference to the world around him or her.

First, you will write a two-paragraph report. Use the People Who Changed the World Chart to help you plan what you are going to write.

The first paragraph should be written like a paragraph, not a list of information. It will include the title, the author's name, the publisher's name, and the number of pages. Also, indicate whether the book is from home, school, or the public library.

The second paragraph will answer the questions we all have. What did the person learn or practice as he or she was growing up? What failures or struggles did this person have before he or she was successful? What was this person's main accomplishment? What does this person's accomplishment mean to you? How has it affected your life? How has this person's accomplishment affected the world?

Now you will create a pretend invention of your own. This is something that you think will make the lives of others better. Would it be a "clapper" flashlight that you can find if the electricity goes out? How about some computer program that would search the Internet and find the type of music you like best? Draw a picture or build a model of this great invention.

People Who Changed the World *(cont.)*

Name _____ **People Who Changed the World Chart**

Person's Name

Write about a main accomplishment here.

Write about any struggles here.

Write about what this accomplishment means to you here.

How has his or her accomplishment affected you or the world?

Picture Stories

Materials

- Picture Stories Planning Page (page 67)
- construction paper
- art supplies such as colored pens, colored pencils, crayons

Procedure

Have you heard the expression "a picture is worth a thousand words"? It means that sometimes a picture can instantly "tell" you something that would take many words to describe. For this book report, you are going to have a great opportunity to prove this.

Use the Picture Stories Planning Page to brainstorm the information from the book that you will need to illustrate—the main character, setting, problem, and solution.

Now take out a piece of construction paper. At the top of the page, write your name, the title of the book, the author's name, and the publisher's name. Then draw four boxes down the page. Leave space next to the boxes for writing.

In the boxes, draw pictures that represent the information you filled out on the Picture Stories Planning Page. Next to the drawings, write a sentence or two about what you drew.

Here's what your page should look like:

Describe the main character.

_____

_____

_____

Describe the setting.

_____

_____

_____

Describe the problem.

_____

_____

_____

Describe how the problem was solved.

_____

_____

_____

Picture Stories *(cont.)*

Name _____ **Picture Stories Planning Page**

Fill in the information in each box.

Character (Who)	Setting (time, place, where?)
_____	_____
_____	_____
_____	_____
_____	_____
_____	_____
_____	_____
_____	_____

Problem (conflict)	Solution (resolution)
_____	_____
_____	_____
_____	_____
_____	_____
_____	_____
_____	_____

Picture Walk

Materials

- Sequence Chart (page 69)

- construction paper

- art supplies such as colored pens, colored pencils, and crayons

Procedure

It's nice to take a walk to look at interesting things. Better yet is when you walk with a friend and you get to show him or her something you really think is great. For this book report you are going to take the class on a walk through your book. Your job is to let the class see the story as you saw it.

Think of the key points in the story that you read. These should be evenly spread throughout the story. You might just decide to have only a beginning, middle, and end. Use the Sequence Chart to help you think of these points.

Use a full piece of construction paper for your report. At the top, write your name, the title, the author's name, and the publisher's name. Lengthwise across your paper, draw lines that look something like the ones in the example at the bottom of the page. You will be drawing in these boxes, so you can make as many as you want, but don't make the page look cluttered.

In each section, draw a picture of your favorite point or event. This picture should be bold and bright. Start with light pencil lines and make the picture take up most of the available room. Next, color your drawings. A good way to check what you've done is to look at your picture from across the room. Can you easily read it? Does it look interesting? Are the pictures too small? This helps you see what others see.

Picture Walk *(cont.)*

Name _____ **Sequence Chart**

List steps or events in time order.

Topic
First
Next
Next
Next
Next
Next
Next
Last

Pop-Up

Teacher Note: This report should be done on a fiction book.

Materials

- Pop-Up Web (page 71)
- construction paper
- scissors
- glue
- art supplies such as colored pens, colored pencils, or crayons

Procedure

For this book report, you will choose any fiction book you would like and describe it by creating a pop-up scene. Your report will include a summary of the story, and information about the book's characters, setting, problem, and solution.

Use the Pop-Up Web to plan the summary and book information that you are going to write.

Using the directions below, build your report.

1. Fold a piece of construction paper in half widthwise.

2. Along the folded edge, cut slits of equal length for the tabs.

3. Open the paper up and gently pull each of the pop-up tabs forward.

4. Take out another piece of construction paper. Draw characters or objects related to the subject or setting of your book. Cut these characters or objects out.

5. With your paper open, glue the characters or objects to the pop-up tabs.

6. At the bottom of the paper, draw lines that you can write on. Write the title of the book, the author's name, and the publisher's name. Then write your summary, information about the characters, the setting, the problem, and the solution.

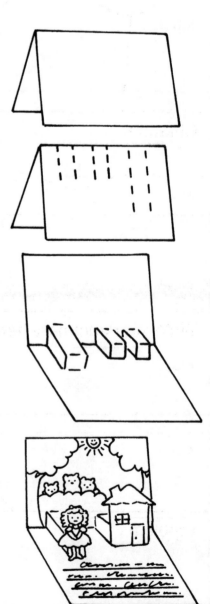

Pop-Up *(cont.)*

Name _____ **Pop-Up Web**

Write words to describe the characters in these circles.

Characters

Characters

Write your summary here.

Problem

Solution

Postcard

Materials

- Postcard Planning Page (page 73)

- 6" x 9" piece of construction paper

- art supplies such as colored pens, colored pencils, or crayons

Procedure

For this book report you are going to pretend to be one of the characters in the book of your choice. You are going to send a postcard from the character to your teacher.

Use the Postcard Planning Page to brainstorm ideas for your postcard.

On a 6" x 9" piece of construction paper, draw one scene from the story. This should show where or when the story takes place and one thing that happened in the story.

Turn over the paper. Draw a line down the middle of the page.

On the left-hand side of the page, write a letter to your teacher that explains your picture. Remember to write as if you are the character in the book. Write to your teacher as if he or she does not know anything about the book. After he or she reads your postcard, your teacher should know something about the story.

Write the address of your school on the right-hand side of the page so that your postcard can be delivered. Be sure to draw a stamp in the upper right hand corner.

Message

Address

_____

_____

_____

_____

Postcard *(cont.)*

Name _____ **Postcard Planning Page**

Title of Book _____

Write about the character here:

Write about the setting here:

Practice drawing your postcard here:

Press Conference

Materials

- Press Conference Planning Page (page 75)
- scissors

Procedure

You may have seen press conferences on TV. Sometimes they are given by the President or another government official, sometimes by people who are well-known in your community, and sometimes even by sports players. When a person gives a press conference, other people get to ask him or her questions about a topic.

With this book report, you are going to give a press conference about your book. Before you do that, you are going to talk to your family or friends and tell them about the story, then have them ask you questions. But you aren't going to answer the questions until you give your press conference to the class. Write the questions down on your Press Conference Planning Page. Make sure that you know the answers!

You should have different types of questions that require you to:

- Tell one reason why we should read this book.
- Define a new word you found in this book.
- Describe one character in the book.
- Describe something you mentioned in the story.
- Solve a new problem using what you learned.
- Wonder what would have to be different if something hadn't occurred.
- Decide if the characters in the book seemed to like each other
- Decide which character was really necessary to the story.

Cut out the questions from the page. Right before your press conference, hand them out to different members of the class. Then you will give a short oral report, including in your report the title of the book, the author's name, and some brief information about the story. When you have finished your report, the class will ask you the questions you prepared. You should answer these and any other questions that the class might have.

Press Conference *(cont.)*

Name _____ **Press Conference Planning Page**

Write the questions below. If you have more, write them on another piece of paper.

1.

2.

3.

4.

5.

6.

7.

Report Card

Teacher Note: This report should be done on a book that has only one main character.

Materials

- Report Card Chart (page 77)

Procedure

For this book report you may choose any book that has only one main character. You are going to create a report card, grading the character on his or her behavior. You will make it look as much like a real report card as you can.

First, decide which behaviors you want to grade. They might include:

- Having a positive attitude
- Following directions
- Helping others
- Thinking of others
- Paying attention
- Assuming and carrying through responsibilities

Take out your Report Card Chart and list the behaviors that you are going to grade. Then grade each one with an A, B, C, D, or F. (You can include minus and plus if you want.)

Beside the grade, write your comments. Why do you think the character deserves that grade? What did the character do in the story to deserve it?

Title of Book ___The Westing Game___   Author ___Ellen Raskin___

Name of Character: ___Turtle Wexler___

Grade your character below.

Behavior	Grade	Comments
Having a positive attitude	C	She kicked anyone who pulled her braid.
Following directions	C	She played the stock market, which wasn't in the game's directions.
Helping others	B	She took the blame for her sister.
Thinking of others	A	She always took care of her friends, including Sandy and Mrs. Baumbach.
Paying attention	A	She solved the mystery
Assuming and carrying through responsibilities	A	She became a very powerful lawyer.

76

Report Card *(cont.)*

Report Card Chart

Name _____

Title of Book _____

Author _____

Name of Character: _____

Grade your character below.

Behavior	Grade	Comments

Scrapbook

Materials

- Scrapbook Planning Page (page 79)

- a scrapbook or bound notebook with a cover and at least four pages

- art supplies such as colored pens, colored pencils, or crayons

Procedure

In this book report, you will focus on the life of the main character of your book. Your report will take the form of a scrapbook. You are going to create the scrapbook as if the character put it together.

Use the Scrapbook Planning Page to plan what you will include in your scrapbook.

The cover of your scrapbook should include the character's name, the title of the book, the author's name, and your name. Use your art supplies to design a colorful, creative cover.

On the first page of the scrapbook, write a letter from the main character to one of the other characters in the book.

On the second page, draw, create, or collect at least four souvenirs that the main character would have put into a scrapbook. The objects should reflect events in the story or important things about the main character.

On the third page, write a diary entry from the main character's point of view. This entry should describe how the main character feels about himself or herself, and how he or she has changed during the story.

On the fourth page, draw a picture of the main character.

Ramond, the Pest!

Scrapbook *(cont.)*

Name _____ **Scrapbook Chart**

Add details to each column.

List of things you will include in the			
Letter	Souvenirs	Diary Entry	Other Things

Sports Trading Card

Materials

- Sports Trading Card Planning Page (page 81)

- 8 ½" x 11" sheet of construction paper

- art supplies such as colored pens, colored pencils, or crayons

Procedure

For this report, you will read a biography about a sports figure. Some of the most interesting people to read about are sports figures. They have usually done some really interesting things in their lives. It's fun to read about them and collect their trading cards. In this book report you will make a trading card to share with the class.

Use the Sports Trading Card Planning Page to record information from the book about your sports figure.

Use the 8 ½" x 11" sheet of construction paper to design your card. Design the team logo or an individual logo and draw the person's picture on one side. On the other side include the statistics from his or her career.

Follow the sample guide below.

| Personal history _____

 _____

 Statistics:

 _____

 _____

 _____

 _____

 Your Name

 _____ | Player's Name_____

 Title _____

 Author _____

 Draw Picture Here |

Sports Trading Card *(cont.)*

Name _____ **Sports Trading Card Planning Page**

Name	
Sport	
League Name	
Team Name	
Position Played	
Awards or Honors Won	

	Personal Average	Sport Average
Points Scored		
Most Points Scored in a game/Match		
Average Score		
Rating		

Story Flag

Materials

- Story Flag Planning Page (page 83)
- construction paper
- art supplies such as colored pens, colored pencils, or crayons

Procedure

You know that countries have flags, but did you know that there are flags for a lot of different things? States, cities, groups, and even certain occasions will have their own flags. Why not create a flag for your book?

Practice some ideas for your flag using the Story Flag Planning Page. Try drawing your favorite part of the book.

Use a full piece of construction paper for your creation. Draw lines to make it look like the sample at the bottom of the page. At the top, write the title and author's name. On one side list all the characters, and on the other, describe the setting. At the bottom of the flag describe your favorite part. Also write your name and the date.

Your picture should be bold and bright. Start with light pencil lines and make the picture take up most of the available room. Next think about the colors. A good way to check if you like what you've done is to look at your flag from across the room. Can you easily read it? Does it look interesting? Are there too many colors? These things can either make your flag look great or cluttered.

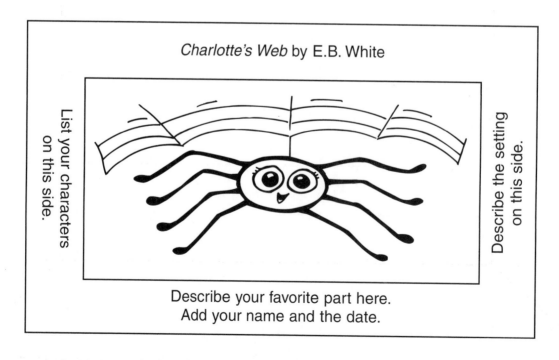

Charlotte's Web by E.B. White

List your characters on this side.

Describe the setting on this side.

Describe your favorite part here.
Add your name and the date.

Story Flag *(cont.)*

Name _____ **Story Flag Planning Page**

Practice on the sample flag below.

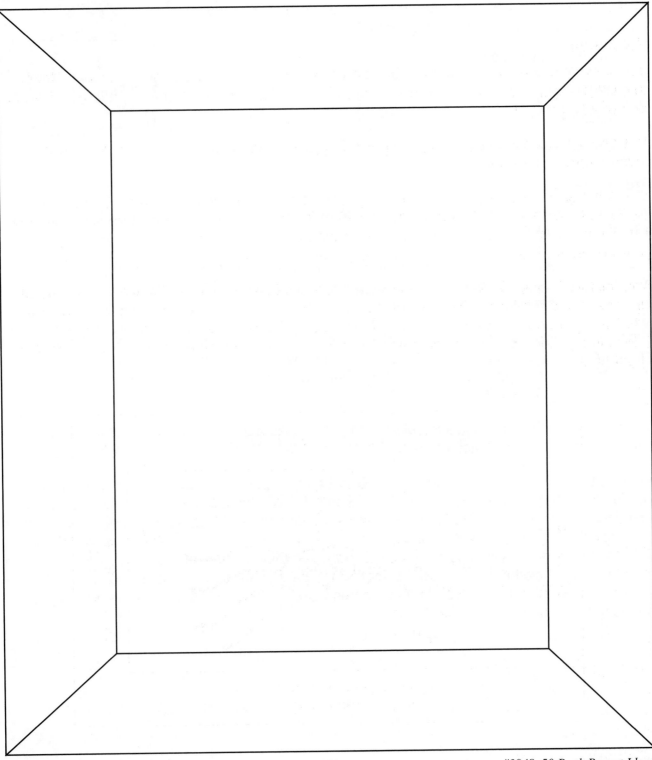

Idea # 41

A Suitcase of Memories

Teacher Note: This report is for a fiction or nonfiction book that takes place in another country.

Materials

- Suitcase of Memories Chart (page 85)
- small box (like a shoebox)
- paper
- scissors
- art supplies such as colored pens, colored pencils, or crayons

Procedure

You are going to read a book that takes place in a faraway location. This might be a fiction or a nonfiction book.

First, you are going to describe where the story took place and what the setting was like. On a separate piece of paper, describe in what ways the location of the story was like your own town and in what ways it was different.

Next, think—if you went to this place what special things would you bring along? Would you need an extra large hat, a map in English, or some favorite food they wouldn't have? Add these items to your Suitcase of Memories Chart. Use words and pictures. Be ready to explain your choices to the class.

Then, make a miniature suitcase out of a small box (like a shoe box). Cut out the items you wrote down on your Suitcase of Memories Chart. "Pack" these items in your suitcase.

Also, write on your Suitcase of Memories Chart a list of people for whom you will want to buy souvenirs. What would you get for each person? Think about what things you might buy in that country. If you are going to Mexico, would you like to buy a beautiful piñata? If your story took place in Japan, would you think about getting a beautiful kimono? What would you buy in France or Turkey? What comes to mind when you think back over the story? Is there some food, a piece of clothing, or possibly something to put in your house that you remember? Write down what you would buy for each person beside his or her name. Good luck with your shopping!

A Suitcase of Memories *(cont.)*

Name _____**Suitcase of Memories Chart**

Possible Souvenirs to take with you	List of People to Buy Souvenirs for	Possible Souvenirs for Those People

Tangrams

Materials

- Tangram Puzzle Pattern (page 87)
- paper
- scissors
- glue

Procedure

The Chinese had puzzles that they called *Tangrams*. These were squares that were cut into seven shapes. Each piece was called a *tan*. For this book report, you will cut out the Tangram Puzzle Pattern and use the shapes to create a picture of a person, animal, or object from your story.

First, you will write a two-paragraph report. The first paragraph should be written like a paragraph, not a list of information. It will include the title, author's name, and publisher's name, as well as the number of pages. Also, indicate whether the book is from home, school, or the public library.

The second paragraph will describe the person, animal, or object you have chosen to create. Why did you choose this person, animal, or object and how was he/she/it important to the story?

Finally, at the bottom of the page, paste the figure you created with the tan pieces. Try to use all seven and place them so they touch each other without overlapping.

Tangrams *(cont.)*

Name _____ **Tangram Puzzle Pattern**

These are sample figures to look at. Cut out the pattern below to make your own tangram design. Move the pieces around to create the shape of a person, object, or animal. Good luck!

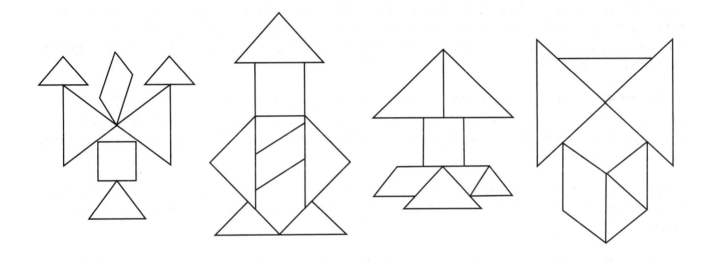

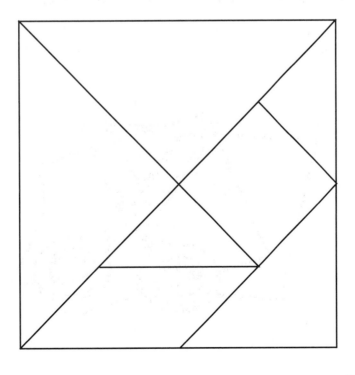

Three-Dimensional Setting

Teacher Note: This report is for a book with a very important and obvious setting. A picture book would be a good choice.

Materials

- 3-D Setting Chart (page 89)
- old newspapers
- Tempera paint
- wallpaper paste (or flour and water)
- recycled objects such as milk cartons, empty cans, or inflated balloons
- paintbrush
- corrugated cardboard for the base no bigger than 12" x 18"

Procedure

This book must be one where the setting is very obvious. A picture book works very well because you are going to build a 3-D map of where the story takes place. Give yourself several days to do this since you will use paste and it will have to dry.

Decide what setting you want to create. Draw it on your 3-D Setting Chart so you can refer back to it. Find used items to create houses, buildings, hills, etc. Milk cartons, boxes, empty cans, and even inflated balloons work well. Arrange and tape them to a cardboard base no bigger than 12" x 18". Next, tear newspaper into long, thin strips. Pour wallpaper paste into a bowl and pull the strips through it, squeezing off the extra paste.

Start laying the newspaper strips down on your scene carefully. Make sure all the sides lay down flat. It helps if you lay them down in one direction.

Repeat the process a total of four times. Once the scene is dry, you can paint it and include anything else you would like. How about adding trees, people, animals, or other objects? The more details you add the more interesting it will be to the class.

You will be presenting your book report to the whole class and explaining what your scene shows.

Three-Dimensional Setting *(cont.)*

Name _____ **3-D Setting Chart**

Use this area to decide where you want to put the buildings, roads, hills, etc.

Time Capsule

Teacher Note: This report is for a book that takes place in the past.

Materials

- Time Capsule Chart (page 91)
- paper
- shoebox
- five items that didn't exist during the time frame of the book

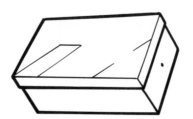

Procedure

For this book report you may choose a fiction or nonfiction book that takes place in the past. After you have read the book, think about what was different about the way the characters lived. Did their homes, means of transportation, or the way they dressed look different to you? How about the things they used or even the way they treated one another? Did this seem strange to you? Write on your Time Capsule Chart how life was then compared to how life is now.

On a separate piece of paper, write a letter to the characters in your book explaining what was different to you about the way they lived and explain to them what your life is like today.

Did you know that the way you live might seem just as strange 100 or 200 years from now? Do you think people will dress the same way, drive cars like ours, or perhaps still eat breakfast cereal? Imagine what it would be like if someone from the future presented you with a time capsule of things that you had never seen before.

Next, you will create a time capsule of at least five items chosen from your home that those people probably wouldn't have seen. This could include a tooth brush, a ball point pen, or an egg timer. Whatever you choose it must fit into a shoe box . Next, write on your Time Capsule Chart a list of those five things and explain why you chose them, why they are significant to you now, and how you use them. What did people do before they had these things?

You will present your report to the class.

Time Capsule *(cont.)*

Name _____**Time Capsule Chart**

How was it then?	How is it now?

What did you pack?	Why did you pack it in your time capsule?

Tissue Box

Teacher Note: This report is for a fiction book.

Materials

- Tissue Box Planning Page (page 93)

- tissue box

- paper

- scissors

- glue

- art supplies such as colored pens, colored pencils, or crayons

Procedure

You get to choose any fiction book you'd like for this report. You are going to illustrate four scenes from the book on the sides of a tissue box. Use your Tissue Box Planning Page to plan the scenes you would like to draw.

Take out your tissue box and glue paper around it to cover it. Around the sides, draw the four scenes that you planned.

Write your name, the book title, the author's name, and the publisher's name on the top of the box.

Once you have created your box, you will be responsible for showing it to the class and explaining your story.

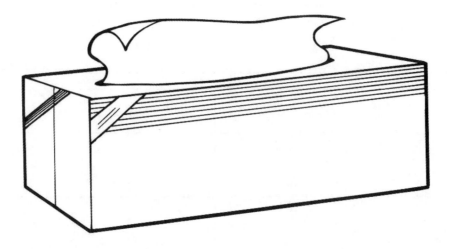

Tissue Box *(cont.)*

Name _____**Tissue Box Planning Page**

Draw the story scenes in these boxes:

Side 1

Side 2

Side 3

Side 4

Idea # 46

T-Shirt Stories

Teacher Note: This report is for a book that is a collection of short stories.

Materials

- T-Shirt Planning Page (page 95)

- stiff cardboard

- paper

- white t-shirt

- crayons

Procedure

For this book report you may choose a book with a collection of short stories. You are going to present your book report on a t-shirt.

Use the T-Shirt Planning Page to plan what you are going to draw on your t-shirt. Draw a scene or a favorite character from each short story.

Take out your real t-shirt and slip it over a stiff piece of cardboard. This will hold the shirt in place for you while you are drawing. Using crayons, draw the scenes you planned on the t-shirt.

On a separate piece of paper, write a short summary of the stories for your presentation. A summary is a retelling of the story. This doesn't mean you include everything, just the key points. Think to yourself, what was that story mostly about? What things do I have to tell to make sure everyone understands what happened? You will be using this summary to help you present your t-shirt in front of the class. Good luck!

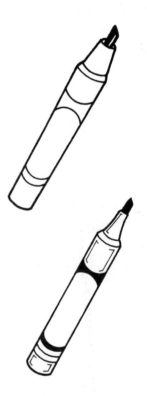

T-Shirt Stories *(cont.)*

Name _____**T-Shirt Planning Page**

Practice on this t-shirt.

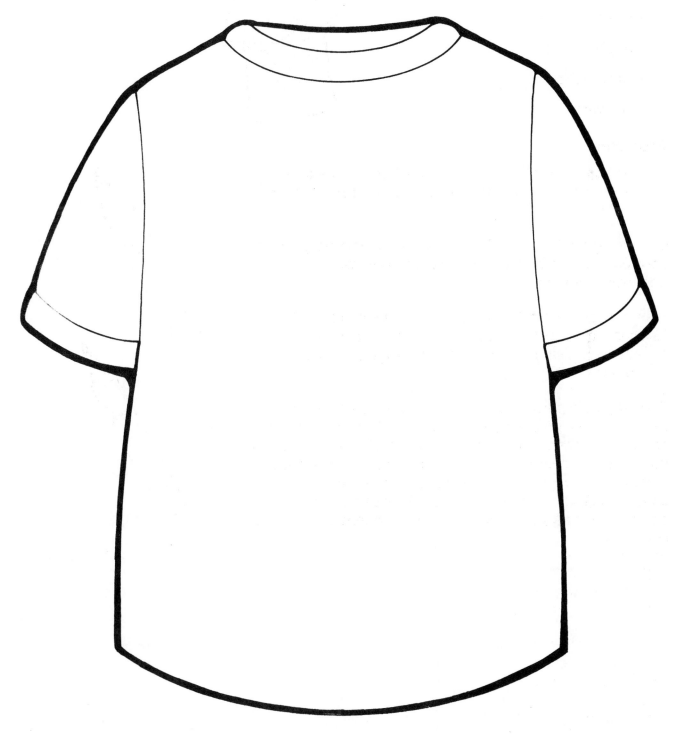

Vanity License Plate

Teacher Note: This report is for a book with different characters in it.

Materials

- Vanity Plate Planning Page (page 97)
- construction paper
- magic markers

Procedure

For this book report you may choose a book with different characters in it.

If you look at cars around town, you will see that the license plates are all different. Some just have letters and numbers that don't mean anything in particular. Some people pay to have vanity license plates that spell out something that is important to the driver. Some of them spell out a simple description of the person who owes the car. Most of them are funny. For this report, you will create these kind of vanity license plates to describe each of the book's main characters.

Figure out how many characters in the book deserve to have their own license plates. Use the Vanity Plate Planning Page to practice some vanity plates for the characters. Each vanity plate should have no more than seven letters or numbers. Use all capital letters and don't leave any spaces between them. Part of the fun of reading vanity plates is trying to figure out what they are saying

Take out a large piece of construction paper. At the top, write the title of the book, the author's name, the publisher's name, and your name. Using a wide magic marker, create vanity plates that are approximately 6" wide and 3" tall. Beneath the license plate, write the character's name. Here are some examples:

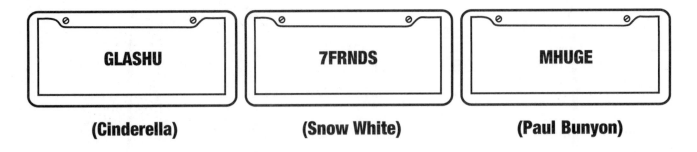

GLASHU	7FRNDS	MHUGE
(Cinderella)	**(Snow White)**	**(Paul Bunyon)**

When you present this to the class it will be their job to try to read them as character descriptions, not just a collection of letters and numbers.

Name _____ **Vanity Plate Graphic**

Practice your vanity plate ideas here.

W-W-W Chart

Teacher Note: This report is for a book on a subject the student would like to know more about.

Materials

- W-W-W Chart (page 99)

Procedure

Choose a book on a subject that you would like to know more about. This book report will help you think about what you know, what you would like to find out, and what you actually learned after you finished the book.

Before you start reading the book, take out your W-W-W Chart page. Some call this kind of chart a K-W-L chart; some call it the W-W-W chart.

In the "What I Already Know" section, write the ideas you have on the subject before you read the book.

In the "What I Want to Know" section, write what you would like to learn from the book.

Read the book. When you have finished, take out your W-W-W Chart page again. The final section of the chart is titled "What I Learned." Think about what you learned from this book and write that information there.

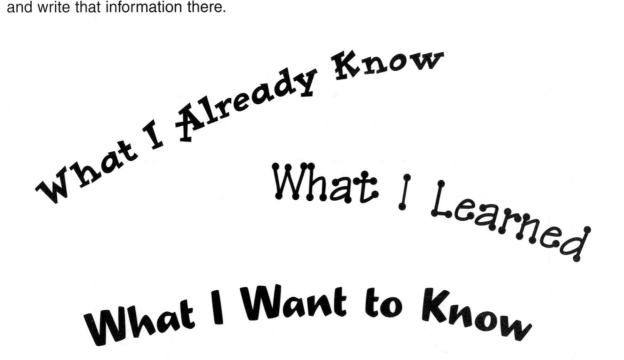

W-W-W Chart *(cont.)*

Name _____**W-W-W Chart**

- Before you read your book, list details in the first two columns.
- Fill in the last column after you read your book.

Topic:
Title:
Author:

What I Already Know	What I Want to Know	What I Learned

Winter Ornament

Teacher Note: This report should be on a fiction book.

Materials

- Winter Ornament Planning Page (page 101)

- item such as a tin can, plastic bottle, or Styrofoam ball to use as the ornament's base

- material such as paper, yarn, or cloth

- art supplies such as paint, colored pens, or crayons

- writing paper

Procedure

You will be making a winter ornament to hang in our room that shows a scene or main character from the book you read. Use your Winter Ornament Planning Page to review words describing the setting and words describing the main character to help you think of ideas for your ornament.

Choose an item such as a tin can, plastic bottle, or Styrofoam ball to be the base for your decoration. Use paper, cloth, yarn, or anything else you can think of, to cover the base. Use paint, colored pens, or crayons to decorate the ornament in a way that represents the story.

This report will also have three written paragraphs. The first one simply tells the name of the book, the author's name, the publisher's name, the number of pages, and where you got the book.

In the second paragraph describe the setting in your story as well as you can. Make anyone who reads the paragraph see and feel the scene just as if he or she was reading the book.

In the final paragraph, describe the main character in a way that makes anyone who reads the paragraph feel like he or she knows the character.

Winter Ornament

Name _____Winter Ornament Planning Page

Words Describing the Setting	Words Describing the Main Character

Your Movie Poster

Materials

- Movie Poster Planning Page (page 103)

- 9" x 12" construction paper

- art supplies such as colored pens, colored pencils, or crayons

Procedure

You can write this report on any book you would like.

Pretend you are going to make a movie of your book. Think about which actors you will cast as the book characters and create a poster to advertise your movie. With that in mind, what kind of movie poster would your book have? What colors would you use to show the mood of the story? What picture would you use that would sell it to all those moviegoers you know?

Use the Movie Poster Planning Page to plan some ideas for your poster.

Take out your 9" x 12" piece of construction paper. Add the title of the book first. The title should be the most prominent part of the poster. List the actors who will play the characters. List your name as the director. Draw your design lightly in pencil first, then add colors that you can easily read from across the room.

Remember to make your poster look fun and exciting. You're trying to get the rest of the class to want to see your movie. Since you are presenting this in front of the class, you will want your movie to seem like a blockbuster. Good luck!

Your Movie Poster *(cont.)*

Name _____ **Movie Poster Planning Page**

Use this chart to help you plan your movie poster. You can change it any way you'd like.

Name of Picture	
Starring	
Director	

Draw your picture here

Parent Consent Form

Parents, Please Sign and Return

Name of Student _____

Book Report Due _____

Name of Book _____

Questions _____

_____

_____

Parent's Signature _____

Book Log

Title of Book   Date Read

_____   _____

_____   _____

_____   _____

_____   _____

_____   _____

_____   _____

_____   _____

_____   _____

_____   _____

_____   _____

_____   _____

Suggested Books—
Newbery Award Winners

Kira-Kira by Cynthia Kadohata (Atheneum Books for Young Readers/Simon & Schuster)

The Tale of Despereaux: Being the Story of a Mouse, a Princess, Some Soup, and a Spool of Thread by Kate DiCamillo, illustrated by Timothy Basil Ering (Candlewick Press)

Crispin: The Cross of Lead by Avi (Hyperion Books for Children)

A Single Shard by Linda Sue Park (YA)

A Year Down Yonder by Richard Peck

Bud, Not Buddy by Christopher Paul Curtis (Delacorte)

Holes by Louis Sachar (Frances Foster)

Out of the Dust by Karen Hesse (Scholastic)

The View from Saturday by E.L. Konigsburg (Jean Karl/Atheneum)

The Midwife's Apprentice by Karen Cushman (Clarion)

Walk Two Moons by Sharon Creech (HarperCollins)

The Giver by Lois Lowry (Houghton)

Missing May by Cynthia Rylant (Jackson/Orchard)

Shiloh by Phyllis Reynolds Naylor (Atheneum)

Maniac Magee by Jerry Spinelli (Little, Brown)

Number the Stars by Lois Lowry (Houghton)

Joyful Noise: Poems for Two Voices by Paul Fleischman (Harper)

Lincoln: A Photobiography by Russell Freedman (Clarion)

The Whipping Boy by Sid Fleischman (Greenwillow)

Sarah, Plain and Tall by Patricia MacLachlan (Harper)

The Hero and the Crown by Robin McKinley (Greenwillow)

Dear Mr. Henshaw by Beverly Cleary (Morrow)

Dicey's Song by Cynthia Voigt (Atheneum)

A Visit to William Blake's Inn: Poems for Innocent and Experienced Travelers by Nancy Willard (Harcourt)

Jacob Have I Loved by Katherine Paterson (Crowell)

A Gathering of Days: A New England Girl's Journal, 1830-1832 by Joan W. Blos (Scribner)

The Westing Game by Ellen Raskin (Dutton)

Bridge to Terabithia by Katherine Paterson (Crowell)

Roll of Thunder, Hear My Cry by Mildred D. Taylor (Dial)

The Grey King by Susan Cooper (McElderry/Atheneum)

M. C. Higgins, the Great by Virginia Hamilton (Macmillan)

The Slave Dancer by Paula Fox (Bradbury)

Julie of the Wolves by Jean Craighead George (Harper)

Mrs. Frisby and the Rats of NIMH by Robert C. O'Brien (Atheneum)

Summer of the Swans by Betsy Byars (Viking)

Sounder by William H. Armstrong (Harper)

The High King by Lloyd Alexander (Holt)

From the Mixed-Up Files of Mrs. Basil E. Frankweiler by E. L. Konigsburg (Atheneum)

Up a Road Slowly by Irene Hunt (Follett)

Suggested Books—
Newbery Award Winners *(cont.)*

I, Juan de Pareja by Elizabeth Borton de Trevino (Farrar)

Shadow of a Bull by Maia Wojciechowska (Atheneum)

It's Like This, Cat by Emily Neville (Harper)

A Wrinkle in Time by Madeleine L'Engle (Farrar)

The Bronze Bow by Elizabeth George Speare (Houghton)

Island of the Blue Dolphins by Scott O'Dell (Houghton)

Onion John by Joseph Krumgold (Crowell)

The Witch of Blackbird Pond by Elizabeth George Speare (Houghton)

Rifles for Watie by Harold Keith (Crowell)

Miracles on Maple Hill by Virginia Sorenson (Harcourt)

Carry On, Mr. Bowditch by Jean Lee Latham (Houghton)

The Wheel on the School by Meindert DeJong (Harper)

. . . And Now Miguel by Joseph Krumgold (Crowell)

Secret of the Andes by Ann Nolan Clark (Viking)

Ginger Pye by Eleanor Estes (Harcourt)

Amos Fortune, Free Man by Elizabeth Yates (Dutton)

The Door in the Wall by Marguerite de Angeli (Doubleday)

King of the Wind by Marguerite Henry (Rand McNally)

The Twenty-One Balloons by William Pène du Bois (Viking)

Miss Hickory by Carolyn Sherwin Bailey (Viking)

Strawberry Girl by Lois Lenski (Lippincott)

Rabbit Hill by Robert Lawson (Viking)

Johnny Tremain by Esther Forbes (Houghton)

Adam of the Road by Elizabeth Janet Gray (Viking)

The Matchlock Gun by Walter Edmonds (Dodd)

Call It Courage by Armstrong Sperry (Macmillan)

Daniel Boone by James Daugherty (Viking)

Thimble Summer by Elizabeth Enright (Rinehart)

The White Stag by Kate Seredy (Viking)

Roller Skates by Ruth Sawyer (Viking)

Caddie Woodlawn by Carol Ryrie Brink (Macmillan)

Dobry by Monica Shannon (Viking)

Invincible Louisa: The Story of the Author of Little Women by Cornelia Meigs (Little, Brown)

Young Fu of the Upper Yangtze by Elizabeth Lewis (Winston)

Waterless Mountain by Laura Adams Armer (Longmans)

The Cat Who Went to Heaven by Elizabeth Coatsworth (Macmillan)

Hitty, Her First Hundred Years by Rachel Field (Macmillan)

The Trumpeter of Krakow by Eric P. Kelly (Macmillan)

Gay Neck, the Story of a Pigeon by Dhan Gopal Mukerji (Dutton)

Moky, the Cowhorse by Will James (Scribner)

Shen of the Sea by Arthur Bowie Chrisman (Dutton)

Tales from Silver Lands by Charles Finger (Doubleday)

The Dark Frigate by Charles Hawes (Little, Brown)

The Voyages of Doctor Dolittle by Hugh Lofting (Lippincott)

The Story of Mankind by Hendrik Willem van Loon (Liveright)

Suggested Books—
California Young Reader Medal Winners

Muncha! Muncha! Muncha! by Candace Fleming and G. Brian Karas (Atheneum Books for Young Readers, 2002)

Ruby Holler by Sharon Creech (Joanna Cotler, 2002)

Things Not Seen by Andrew Clements (Philomel Books, 2002)

Stormbreaker by Anthony Horowitz (Philomel Books, 2001)

Mr. Lincoln's Way by Patricia Polacco (Philomel, 2001)

A Fine, Fine School by Sharon Creech (HarperCollins, 2001)

The School Story by Andrew Clements (Simon & Schuster, 2001)

Flipped by Wendelin Van Draanen (Knopf, 2001)

Ties That Bind, Ties That Break by Lensey Namioka (Delacorte Press, 1999)

And the Dish Ran Away With the Spoon by Janet Stevens (Harcourt, 2001)

I Will Never, Not Ever Eat a Tomato by Lauren Child (Candlewick, 2000)

Because of Winn Dixie by Kate DiCamillo (Candlewick, 2000)

Touching Spirit Bear by Ben Mikaelsen (HarperCollins, 2001)

Define "Normal" by Julie Anne Peters (Little Brown, 2000)

The Babe and I by David Adler (Harcourt Brace, 1999)

Hooway for Wodney Wat by Helen Lester. Illustrated by Lynn Munsinger (Houghton Mifflin, 1999)

Million Dollar Shot by Dan Gutman (Hyperion, 1997)

Joey Pigza Swallowed the Key by Jack Gantos (Farrar, Straus & Giroux, 1998)

Bad by Jean Ferris (Farrar, Straus, and Giroux, 1998)

Weslandia by Paul Fleischman (Candlewick, 1999)

Grandpa's Teeth by Rod Clement (HarperCollins, 1998)

Honus and Me: A Baseball Card Adventure by Dan Gutman (Avon, 1997)

Among the Hidden by Margaret Peterson Haddix (Simon & Schuster, 1998)

Armageddon Summer by Jane Yolen and Bruce Coville (Harcourt Brace, 1998)

Lost by Paul Brett Johnson and Celeste Lewis (Orchard, 1996)

Riding Freedom by Pam Munoz Ryan (Scholastic, 1999)

Ella Enchanted by Gail Carson Levine (Harper Trophy, 1998)

Breaking Boxes by A.M. Jenkins (Bantam Doubleday Dell, 1998)

The 13th Floor: A Ghost Story by Sid Fleischman. Illustrated by Peter Sis (Greenwillow Press, 1995)

Under the Blood-Red Sun by Graham Salisbury (Delacorte Press, 1994)

The Only Alien on the Planet by Kristen Randle (Scholastic, 1995)

Dog Breath by Dav Piley (Blue Sky Press, 1994)

The Junkyard Dog by Erika Tamar (Knopf, 1995)

The Watsons Go to Birmingham by Christopher Paul Curtis (Delacorte, 1995)

Ironman by Chris Crutcher (Greenwillow, 1995)

Don't Fidget a Feather by Erica Silverman. Illustrated by S.D. Schindler (Macmillan, 1994)

Jennifer Murdley's Toad by Bruce Coville (Harcourt, 1992; Pocket Books, 1993)

Sparrow Hawk Red by Ben Mikaelsen (Hyperion, 1993)

Staying Fat for Sarah Byrnes by Chris Crutcher (Greenwillow, 1993; Dell, 1995)

Suggested Books—
California Young Reader Medal Winners *(cont.)*

Stellaluna by Janell Cannon (Harcourt Brace, 1994)

Time for Andrew: A Ghost Story by Mary Downing Hahn (Clarion Books, 1994)

Freak the Mighty by Rodman Philbrick (Scholastic, 1993)

Shadow of the Dragon by Sherry Garland (Harcourt Brace, 1994)

Martha Speaks by Susan Meddaugh (Houghton, 1992)

Stonewords: A Ghost Story by Pam Conrad (HarperCollins, 1990; 1991)

Rescue John McGuire by Ben Mikaelsen (Hyperion, 1991; 1993)

Downriver by Will Hobbs (Atheneum, 1991; Bantam/Starfire, 1992)

High-Wire Henry by Mary Calhoun. Illustrated by Erick Ingraham (Morrow, 1991)

Scared Stiff by Willo Davis Roberts (Atheneum, 1991)

There's a Girl in My Hammerlock by Jerry Spinelli (Simon & Schuster, 1991; 1993)

We All Fall Down by Robert Cormier (Delacorte, 1991; Dell, 1993)

Julius, the Baby of the World by Kevin Henkes (Greenwillow, 1990; Mulberry Books, 1992)

Fudge-a-Mania by Judy Blume (Dutton, 1990; Dell, 1991)

Something Upstairs by Avi (Orchard, 1988; Avon, 1990)

The Silver Kiss by Annette Curtis Klause (Delacorte, 1990; Dell, 1992)

Never Spit on Your Shoes by Denys Cazet (Clarion, 1986; Orchard Books, 1990)

All About Sam by Lois Lowry (Houghton Mifflin, 1988)

Sniper by Theodore Taylor (Harcourt, Brace, Jovanovich, 1989)

A Sudden Silence by Eve Bunting (Harcourt, Brace, Jovanovich, 1989)

Tacky the Penguin by Helen Lester. Illustrated by Lynn Munsinger (Houghton Mifflin, 1988)

Harry's Mad by Dick King-Smith (Crown, 1987; Dell, 1988)

December Stillness by Mary Downing Hahn (Clarion, 1988)

Night Kites by M.E. Kerr (Harper & Row, 1986)

Eyes of the Dragon by Margaret Leaf. Illustrated by Ed Young (Lothrop, 1987)

The War with Grandpa by Robert K. Smith (Delacourt, 1984)

The Other Side of Dark by Joan Lowery Nixon (Delacorte, 1986; Dell, 1987)

Izzy, Willy Nilly by Cynthia Voigt (Atheneum, 1996; Fawcett, 1987)

What Happened to Patrick's Dinosaurs? by Carol Carrick. Illustrated by Donald Carrick (Clarion, 1986)

The Castle in the Attic by Elizabeth Winthrop (Holiday House, 1985; Bantam, 1986)

The Stalker by Joan Lowery Nixon (Delacorte, 1985)

The Face at the Edge of the World by Eve Bunting (Ticknor, 1985; Dell, 1986)

If You Give a Mouse a Cookie by Laura Joffe Numeroff. Illustrated by Felicia Bond (Harper & Row, 1985; Scholastic, 1988)

Be a Perfect Person in Just 3 Days by Stephen Manes (Houghton Mifflin, 1982; Bantam, 1987)

The Root Cellar by Janet Lunn (Scribner, 1983; Penguin, 1985)

Interstellar Pig by William Sleator (Dutton, 1984)

Suggested Books—
California Young Reader Medal Winners *(cont.)*

The Napping House by Audrey Wood. Illustrated by Don Wood Harcourt Brace, 1984

The Dollhouse Murders by Betty Ren Wright (Holiday House, 1983; Scholastic, 1985)

You Shouldn't Have to Say Goodbye by Patricia Hermes (Harcourt, Brace, Jovanovich, 1982; Scholastic, 1984)

Pursuit by Michael French (Delacorte, 1981; Dell, 1983)

Space Case by Edward Marshall. Illustrated by James Marshall (Dial, 1980)

Nothing's Fair in Fifth Grade by Barthe DeClements (Viking, 1981; Scholastic, 1982)

Girl with the Silver Eyes by Willo Davis Roberts (Atheneum, 1980; Scholastic, 1982)

The Darkangel by Meredith Pierce (Little Brown, 1982; Dell, 1982)

Herbie's Troubles by Carol Chapman. Illustrated by Kelly Oechsli (Dutton, 1981)

The Indian in the Cupboard by Lynne Reid Banks (Doubleday, 1980; Avon, 1982)

Taking Terri Mueller by Norma Fox Mazer (Morrow, 1983; Avon, 1981)

The Truth Trap by Frances Miller (Dutton, 1980; Dell, 1982)

Bagdad At It by Phyllis Green. Illustrated by Joel Schick (Watts, 1980)

The Trouble with Tuck by Theodore Taylor (Doubleday, 1981)

There's a Bat in Bunk Five by Paula Danziger (Delacorte, 1980; Dell, 1982)

Stranger with My Face by Lois Duncan (Little, Brown, 1981; Dell, 1982)

Liza Lou and the Yeller Belly Swamp by Mercer Mayer (Scholastic, 1977)

Superfudge by Judy Blume (Dutton, 1980; Dell, 1981)

Tiger Eyes by Judy Blume (Bradbury, 1981; Dell, 1982)

Summer of Fear by Lois Duncan (Little, Brown, 1976; Dell, 1977)

Miss Nelson is Missing by Harry Allard. Illustrated by James Marshall (Houghton Mifflin, 1977)

Hail, Hail, Camp Timberwood by Ellen Conford (Little, Brown, 1987; Archway, 1980)

Summer of the Monkeys by Wilson Rawls (Doubleday, 1977; Dell 1979)

A Summer to Die by Lois Lowry (Houghton Mifflin, 1977; Bantam, 1979)

Big Bad Bruce by Bill Peet (Houghton Mifflin, 1977)

The Pinballs by Betsy Byars (Harper & Row, 1977)

Danny, the Champion of the World by Roald Dahl (Knopf, 1975)

The Late Great Me by Sandra Scoppettone (Putnam, 1976)

Little Rabbit's Loose Tooth by Lucy Bate. Illustrated by Diane de Groat (Crown, 1975)

Freaky Friday by Mary Rodgers (Harper & Row, 1972)

Watership Down by Richard Adams (Macmillan, 1972)

How Droofus the Dragon Lost His Head by Bill Peet (Houghton Mifflin,

How to Eat Fried Worms by Thomas Rockwell (Watts, 1973)

Suggested Books— Caldecott Medal Winners

Kitten's First Full Moon by Kevin Henkes (Greenwillow Books/HarperCollinsPublishers)

The Man Who Walked Between the Towers by Mordicai Gerstein (Roaring Brook Press/Millbrook Press)

My Friend Rabbit by Eric Rohmann (Roaring Brook Press/Millbrook Press)

The Three Pigs by David Wiesner (Clarion/Houghton Mifflin)

So You Want to Be President? Illustrated by David Small, written by Judith St. George (Philomel)

Joseph Had a Little Overcoat by Simms Taback (Viking)

Snowflake Bentley, Illustrated by Mary Azarian, text by Jacqueline Briggs Martin (Houghton)

Rapunzel by Paul O. Zelinsky (Dutton)

Golem by David Wisniewski (Clarion)

Officer Buckle and Gloria by Peggy Rathmann (Putnam)

Smoky Night, illustrated by David Diaz; text: Eve Bunting (Harcourt)

Grandfather's Journey by Allen Say; text: edited by Walter Lorraine (Houghton)

Mirette on the High Wire by Emily Arnold McCully (Putnam)

Tuesday by David Wiesner (Clarion)

Black and White by David Macaulay (Houghton)

Lon Po Po: A Red-Riding Hood Story from China by Ed Young (Philomel)

Song and Dance Man, illustrated by Stephen Gammell; text: Karen Ackerman (Knopf)

Owl Moon, illustrated by John Schoenherr; text: Jane Yolen (Philomel)

Hey, Al, illustrated by Richard Egielski; text: Arthur Yorinks (Farrar)

The Polar Express by Chris Van Allsburg (Houghton)

Saint George and the Dragon, illustrated by Trina Schart Hyman; text: retold by Margaret Hodges (Little, Brown)

The Glorious Flight: Across the Channel with Louis Bleriot by Alice & Martin Provensen (Viking)

Shadow, translated and illustrated by Marcia Brown Original text in French: Blaise Cendrars (Scribner)

Jumanji by Chris Van Allsburg (Houghton)

Fables by Arnold Lobel (Harper)

Ox-Cart Man, illustrated by Barbara Cooney; text: Donald Hall (Viking)

The Girl Who Loved Wild Horses by Paul Goble (Bradbury)

Noah's Ark by Peter Spier (Doubleday)

Ashanti to Zulu: African Traditions, illustrated by Leo & Diane Dillon; text: Margaret Musgrove (Dial)

Why Mosquitoes Buzz in People's Ears, illustrated by Leo & Diane Dillon; text: retold by Verna Aardema (Dial)

Arrow to the Sun by Gerald McDermott (Viking)

Duffy and the Devil, illustrated by Margot Zemach; retold by Harve Zemach (Farrar)

The Funny Little Woman, illustrated by Blair Lent; text: retold by Arlene Mosel (Dutton)

One Fine Day, retold and illustrated by Nonny Hogrogian (Macmillan)

Suggested Books—
Caldecott Medal Winners *(cont.)*

A Story A Story, retold and illustrated by Gail E. Haley (Atheneum)

Sylvester and the Magic Pebble by William Steig (Windmill Books)

The Fool of the World and the Flying Ship, illustrated by Uri Shulevitz; text: retold by Arthur Ransome (Farrar)

Drummer Hoff, illustrated by Ed Emberley; text: adapted by Barbara Emberley (Prentice-Hall)

Sam, Bangs & Moonshine by Evaline Ness (Holt)

Always Room for One More, illustrated by Nonny Hogrogian; text: Sorche Nic Leodhas, pseud. [Leclair Alger] (Holt)

May I Bring a Friend? illustrated by Beni Montresor; text: Beatrice Schenk de Regniers (Atheneum)

Where the Wild Things Are by Maurice Sendak (Harper)

The Snowy Day by Ezra Jack Keats (Viking)

Once a Mouse, retold and illustrated by Marcia Brown (Scribner)

Baboushka and the Three Kings, illustrated by Nicolas Sidjakov; text: Ruth Robbins (Parnassus)

Nine Days to Christmas, illustrated by Marie Hall Ets; text: Marie Hall Ets and Aurora Labastida (Viking)

Chanticleer and the Fox, illustrated by Barbara Cooney; text: adapted from Chaucer's Canterbury Tales by Barbara Cooney (Crowell)

Time of Wonder by Robert McCloskey (Viking)

A Tree is Nice, illustrated by Marc Simont; text: Janice Udry (Harper)

Frog Went A-Courtin', illustrated by Feodor Rojankovsky; text: retold by John Langstaff (Harcourt)

Cinderella, or the Little Glass Slipper, illustrated by Marcia Brown; text: translated from Charles Perrault by Marcia Brown (Scribner)

Madeline's Rescue by Ludwig Bemelmans (Viking)

The Biggest Bear by Lynd Ward (Houghton)

Finders Keepers, illustrated by Nicolas, pseud. (Nicholas Mordvinoff); text: Will, pseud. [William Lipkind] (Harcourt)

The Egg Tree by Katherine Milhous (Scribner)

Song of the Swallows by Leo Politi (Scribner)

The Big Snow by Berta & Elmer Hader (Macmillan)

White Snow, Bright Snow, illustrated by Roger Duvoisin; text: Alvin Tresselt (Lothrop)

The Little Island, illustrated by Leonard Weisgard; text: Golden MacDonald, pseud. [Margaret Wise Brown] (Doubleday)

The Rooster Crows by Maude & Miska Petersham (Macmillan)

Prayer for a Child, illustrated by Elizabeth Orton Jones; text: Rachel Field (Macmillan)

Many Moons, illustrated by Louis Slobodkin; text: James Thurber (Harcourt)

The Little House by Virginia Lee Burton (Houghton)

Make Way for Ducklings by Robert McCloskey (Viking)

They Were Strong and Good, by Robert Lawson (Viking)

Abraham Lincoln by Ingri & Edgar Parin d'Aulaire (Doubleday)

Mei Li by Thomas Handforth (Doubleday)

Animals of the Bible, A Picture Book, illustrated by Dorothy P. Lathrop; text: selected by Helen Dean Fish (Lippincott)